A
PROPHETIC
VOICE

A
PROPHETIC
VOICE

From New Orleans to the World

ARTHUR GABRIEL TERRANCE

To order additional copies of this book, contact:
Xlibris
1-888-795-4274
www.Xlibris.com
Orders@Xlibris.com
795502

CONTENTS

A Word From The Author

New Orleans, La. has been called, "the city that care forgot" as long as I can remember. However, God has always had a glorious plan of restoration for this great city. A lot of the revelations that the writer received were given to him in the year of 1985. God began to show him that there was coming destruction and a new day of restoration. God speaks to us on the mountaintop and in the valley low. The author will be sharing moments in his life in which he believes that God spoke to him through the scriptures in the Holy Bible from 1979 until today. God speaks to our spirit, soul, heart, will, and emotions by His Word and by His precious Holy Spirit. The Holy Spirit will never make up a new message and pass it off as coming from God. Jesus gives you and I a spiritual map to be able to determine who is speaking to us. In John 16: 13 "Howbeit when he, the Spirit of truth, is come, he will guide you into all truth: for he shall not speak of himself; but whatsoever he shall hear, that shall he speak: and he will show you things to come. 14 He shall glorify me: for he shall receive of mine, and shall show it unto you. 15 All things that the Father hath are mine: therefore said I that he shall take of mine, and shall show it unto you. It is my prayer that your life will be enriched before you finish reading this book. My desire is to be able to stimulate your appetite to purposefully read the bible on a regular basis. Many people in the World desire to know what good can come out of New Orleans, La. I am a living testimony preserved for "such a time like this." God will begin to reveal himself to everyone who seeks him with his or her whole heart. Then you will be able to say with the billions of believers that God lives and the Holy Spirit speaks today!

Acknowledgments

First of all, I would like to thank my three children, Rebekah Nicole, Arthur Josiah, and Jonathan Caleb for their unconditional love and inspiration. Also, I would like to extend a special thanks to my parents- (the late) Melvin Joseph Terrance, Sr., and Marie Ursula Christophe- Terrance, who continually encouraged me to work towards accomplishing my personal dreams. This was the beginning of a God-given vision that led me to pursue Biblical training from 1986-1990 at International Bible College, located in San Antonio, Texas. God put a strong conviction in my heart to publish a book about a future Spiritual Restoration. A lot of perseverance and critic from my friends and strangers motivated me to complete this book. This book is filled with years of testimonies and experiences that I had growing up as a Christian. This book was inspired by life's experiences and by simple faith in God, who is the Creator of the heavens and the earth. The author acknowledges the invaluable input of the following individuals and organizations, in particular those who provided materials and other support during the development of this book directly or in-directly: *All teachers at International Bible College (1986-1990), The King James Bible published in 1611,* **http://www.graceumcdallas. org/historic_grace/pages/pages_haskell/dove.htm**, *(dove photo)* **www. biblegateway.com**, *New American Standard, GOD'S WORD ® Translation, Weymouth New Testament,*

CHAPTER 1

The Conversion-June 14,1979-

The most important call that we all must heed, is the call to except Jesus Christ as Savior and Lord. That famous verse of scripture in the bible can still penetrate to the core of the spirit of man and produce Salvation. John 3:16 "For God so loved the world that He gave His only begotten Son, that whoever believes in Him should not perish but have everlasting life."

I will never forget what literally happened to me whenever I personally invited Jesus Christ into my heart on June 14, 1979. The experience or encounter that I had on that day set the tone for a fervent quest that I have for God. I remember the Sermon and the invitation that was given by the Evangelist to accept Jesus. There was a little bit of fear, because I felt that I was dis-appoint-ing my Catholic family. Will my mom be mad at me for changing my religion?

However, the desire in which I had for God was much stronger than the consequences for deciding to let Jesus Christ come into my heart. I wanted to know God more and more as the days were passing by. The Word of God began to take first place in my life. One hour felt like a few minutes and the days I spent with the Lord were like moments that seemed to come and disappear.

The words below describes what happened to me:

"It happened late one evening when I was old enough to know. Messiah came to save us and bring salvation to our souls. He is the Lamb of God, who took our sins and washed them all away. Now today I have no reason to live a life of sin.I heard about a Savior who desires to live within. So I surrender to you Lord and ask you to come in my heart to stay...today. You're my Jehovah, you're my Creator, my Lord and Savior, the Bright and Morning Star. You're my Jehovah, you're my Creator, my Precious Savior, the King and Lord of all."

I remember how much that the grass, and the leaves on the trees, looked greener and brighter. I wanted to hug and kiss everyone on the day that I accepted Jesus Christ as my personal Savior. A baptism of love and forgiveness began to transform my heart and mind. The anger that I had towards others was no longer in existence. I truly remember thinking that I don't hate anyone. The spirit of love was taking over and I vowed to give Him full control of my life!

The Bible tells us that whenever someone accepts Jesus Christ into their heart by faith in the precious blood of Jesus Christ, that new life will begins to manifest. The old way of thinking and living has changed. Now there is a new spirit, soul, and body. In other words a new person has been born into the family of God.

2 Corinthians 5:17 "Therefore if any man be in Christ, he is a new creature: old things are passed away; behold, all things are become new."

I clearly remember the transformation process that started to take place in my heart and mind. For example: I had an overwhelming desire to want to read and study the Word of God. I did not want to go and do mischievous things with my friends anymore, or say bad words. My mother was very concerned at the beginning of this conversion. A teen-age boy did not want to do normal things. "All of a sudden, you decided to change."

This was one of the early statements or phrases in which many of my close family members and friends used to describe what they were seeing from the outside looking in. I began to attend a particular bible study which God used to lay the foundation of discipleship. I really wanted to follow Jesus Christ of Nazareth. The scriptures were becoming a literal source of spiritual strength to me. This is why I can understand what Jesus was trying to convey to His disciples in regards to being persistent in his teachings.

John 8:31

"Then said Jesus to those Jews which believed on him, If ye continue in my word, then are ye my disciples indeed; 32 And ye shall know the truth, and the truth shall make you free. 33 They answered him, we be Abraham's seed, and were never in bondage to any man: how sayest thou, ye shall be made free? 34 Jesus answered them, Verily, verily, I say unto you; whosoever committeth sin is the servant of sin. 35 And the servant abideth not in the house forever: but the Son abideth ever. 36 If the Son therefore shall make you free, ye shall be free indeed.

I want every Bible–believing citizens of the world to understand one eternal and universal truth: "Jesus knew what he was talking about and he spoke the entire truth of God." The other philosophers never spoke or taught with authority or certainty. But God eternally anointed Jesus' words. All of His words were delivered with the perfect wisdom and knowledge of God. The scholars of Jesus' day marveled at the depth of wisdom in which he possessed.

Whenever you are truly changed by God's word or when this process begins to take place inside of your spirit, heart, soul, and body, then you will never desire to go back to your old way of living. Although temptations will try to deceive us into thinking that perhaps it is better to compromise instead of remaining faithful to God. The same inspiration from the Holy Scriptures that revealed the Son of God to your heart is still able to restore and bless your life today. The Word of God lives and it comforts, rebukes, and guides our lives everyday.

The only way that I was able to see the transforming power of God in my life was through three spiritual structures: 1) weekly Bible Studies, 2) attending church on Sundays and Wednesdays 3) fellowship with believers on a regular basis. Whenever Jesus Christ comes into your heart, he puts a holy desire deep inside of you to talk, walk, and live holy. In the past it was so easy for me to get upset with another individual and speak profanity. But God's Spirit has a job to follow the commands instructions of Jesus Christ.

John 16: 8-11 And when He has come, He will convict the world of sin, righteousness and of judgment: 9 of sin because they believe not in me; 10 of righteousness because I go to my father and you see me no more; 11 of judgment because the prince of this world is judged.

God wants to change us inside out into the very image of His Son. Sanctification is a continual process that should be taking place inside of our hearts twenty-four hours a day. We are in God's washing machine. The detergent that always gets the stain out-is the blood of Jesus Christ. The Apostle Paul seems to emphasize this concept in the book of Titus chapter three, verse five. "5Not by works of righteousness which we have done, but according to his mercy he saved us, by the washing of regeneration, and renewing of the Holy Ghost; 6 which he shed on us abundantly through Jesus Christ our Savior; 7 that being justified by his grace, we should be made heirs according to the hope of eternal life."

Chapter 2

Power In The Word Of God-1983

We shall behold Jesus face to face, one day very soon. All of the questions unanswered on this earth will be known or revealed whenever we stand in His presence. The powers of darkness shall no longer prevail. But the Church will shine like a bright light, which is the standard against darkness. God's people will walk in true holiness and victory in the midst of a wicked and perverse generation. Now we are beginning to know and understand who we are and for what purpose we were born-again into the kingdom of light. Jesus has made us fit to be called the children of light, because we believed in his name.

Philippians 2:5-11 Let this mind be in you, which was also in Christ Jesus: 6 who, being in the form of God, thought it not robbery to be equal with God: 7 But made himself of no reputation, and took upon him the form of a servant, and was made in the likeness of men: 8 And being found in fashion as a man, he humbled himself, and became obedient unto death, even the death of the cross. 9 Wherefore God also hath highly exalted him, and given him a name which is above every name: 10 that at the name of Jesus every knee should bow, of things in heaven, and things in earth, and things under the earth; 11 And that every tongue should confess that Jesus Christ is Lord, to the glory of God the Father."

Since we have also received Christ into our hearts, we automatically became sons and daughters of a living God. Every created being is going to have to bow before the Creator of the heavens and earth and render honor and praise to the One who sits upon His throne. Let the redeemed of the Lord rejoice in the Lord. Never allow your heart to condemn you whenever you fail God or make a mistake. The Holy Spirit will convict us of our sins. Then you and I can confess our sins directly to Jesus Christ and humbly ask him for forgive-ness. Because of the sacrifice that Jesus gave at the cross, God has eternally obligated himself to pardon the sins of the World if they would pray to him in faith in the blood of the 'lamb of God.

1 John 1:7-9 7 But if we walk in the light as he is in the light, we have fellowship one with another and the blood of Jesus Christ his Son cleanses us from all sin. *8* If we say that we have no sin, we deceive ourselves, and the truth is not in us. *9* If we confess our sins, he is faithful and just to forgive us our sins, and to cleanse us from all unrighteousness.

Now you are ready to worship the Lord and walk in fellowship with him by the leadership of the Holy Spirit. It is the power of God's Spirit that gives us the strength to resist sin and obey the Word of God. In the Holy Bible we find instructions to follow him and walk by faith. We learn how walk only where he leads us. The more that we are led by the Holy Spirit, it helps us to recognize that we are the children of God and that He is leading us to a place of victory!

Romans 8: 14 For as many as are led by the Spirit of God, they are the sons of God. In these perilous times, the believer must maintain a strong faith, which comes by knowledge and understanding of the scriptures. Also, we need to have spiritual ears in order to hear what the Spirit is saying to the Church. The Holy Spirit will never tell you to do something that contradicts the Word of God. Whenever, I began to serve the Lord in the early days, it was like a little baby that could not stand on his feet by himself, but needed the support of his mother to teach him how to walk on a daily basis. Now that we know what faith is, we need to strive to always walk by faith in every-thing that we do or say.

1 Corinthians 13:11 When I was a child, I spoke as a child, I understood as a child, I thought as a child: but when I became a man, I put away childish things.

Every living human being has to pass through the birth canal and be delivered into this World through natural birth or by Medical science intervention. However, none of us can brag about knowing how to speak on our first day of existence. We had to be taught phonics and pronunciation of letters, vowels and consonant sounds. Before long about age of two to three years old, some of us were beginning to speak perfect sentences. As we begin to grow in Christ we must put aside "baby talk" and begin to boldly speak and confess who we are in the Lord. Always be ready to stand up for the proclamation of the gospel of Jesus Christ.

It is very important that you fully understand that Jesus gave us power and authority over Satan, the Gates of Hell, demonic forces, sickness, disease, poverty, and over anything that is contrary to complete victory. This authority comes through the name of Jesus Christ. The more we use the name of Jesus Christ; our faith in God becomes stronger. Now you will begin to see the forces of evil moving back.

Psalms 5: 11-12 But let all those that put their trust in thee rejoice: let them ever shout for joy, because thou defendest them: let them also that love thy name be joyful in thee. 12 For thou, LORD, will bless the righteous: with favor will thou compass him as with a shield.

When the Savior Jesus Christ enters into your heart, you will never be the same again. The mention of His name will prompt you to want to fall on your face and worship him, who is forever the King of kings and the Lord of lords. We can certainly put our trust completely in God and trust that He is going to be faithful to keep the promises made to His children. Rejoice and be glad in the Lord. He has done great things and we should praise him in the midst of every trial and test. "Lord, I praise you and thank you that you are in full control. I surrender to your perfect will. Let the Holy Spirit lead and guide me into all truth. I want to know you as Savior, Lord, Teacher, Father, Healer, Forgiver, and the one who blesses his people.

CHAPTER 3

Mood Swings: 1985

Whatever mood you're in will determine what spirit you are in. The choice is ultimately in your hands. God's sweet Holy Spirit cannot stay in the midst of someone who is constantly complaining. The enemy of our souls knows that if he can keep us focused on the problem that we will be unable to be effective in performing the will of God. The sin of murmuring caused many of God's people to be destroyed. We can see how that God is grieved or saddened whenever we engage in this kind of behavior. I would like to challenge all of God's people to come back to the Altar of Prayer and begin to wait on the Lord in reverence.

At one time or another, you and I have complained or murmured just like the children of Israel: we were only seeing the bad things while failing to recognize the goodness and prosperity of the Lord in our lives.

Numbers 16:41-48 But on the next day all the congregation of the sons of Israel grumbled against Moses and Aaron, saying, "You are the ones who have caused the death of the LORD'S people." 42 It came about, however, when the congregation had assembled against Moses and Aaron, that they turned toward the tent of meeting, and behold, the cloud covered it and the glory of the LORD appeared. 43 Then Moses and Aaron came to the front of the tent of meeting, 44 and the LORD spoke to Moses, saying, 45 get you up from among this congregation, that I may consume them as in a moment. And they fell upon their faces.46 Moses said to Aaron, "Take your censer and put in it fire from the altar, and lay incense on it; then bring it quickly to the congregation and make atonement for them, for wrath has gone forth from the LORD, the plague has begun!" consume them instantly." Then they fell on their faces. 47 Then Aaron took it as Moses had spoken, and ran into the midst of the assembly, for behold, the plague had begun among the people. So he put on the incense and made atonement for the people. 48 He took his stand between the dead and the living, so that the plague was checked.

Our hearts seem to become hardened during those trying times in our lives. It takes godly sorrow to break through a stony heart that isn't yielding to the hand of God. Whenever we are broken and contrite before the Lord, we have a genuine desire to want to repent and walk in the perfect will of God. Ask God to forgive you right now. Then allow the Holy Spirit to minister restoration to you. Begin to thank the Lord Jesus for the sacrifice he paid when he was crucified. Tell the Lord how much you love and appreciate his love for you. Now you are in the right mood and your spirit is in the perfect will of God.

We must examine ourselves to see what manner of spirit we are operating in. The Word of God teaches us in the Book of James that sweet and bitter water should not flow from the same fountain. Love and hate should only exist in this order.

Love God and hate the devil. Have a love for obedience and remember that we must never allow a root of bitterness to control us. The cross of Jesus Christ has the power to break all forms of prejudices, discriminations, abuses, and depression.

Luke 9:51 And it came to pass, when the time was come that he should be received up, he steadfastly set his face to go to Jerusalem, 52 And sent messengers before his face: and they went, and entered into a village of the Samaritans, to make ready for him. 53 And they did not receive him, because his face was as though he would go to Jerusalem. 54 And when his disciples James and John saw this, they said, Lord, wilt thou that we command fire to come down from heaven, and consume them, even as Elias did? 55 But he turned, and rebuked them, and said, ye know not what manner of spirit ye are of. 56 For the Son of man is not come to destroy men's lives, but to save them. And they went to another village. Even the twelve disciples that walked with Jesus, the Messiah were faced with obstacles that, needed to be resolved. All of them overcame the temptations except for Judas Iscariot. He was considered to be the Son of Perdition. He refused to rid himself of a personal or spiritual vendetta against Jesus. In the very end, Judas ended up self-destructing. If we can learn to keep our eyes and minds always on Jesus and not on people, we will maintain a right spirit.

The Bible tells us that the time is coming in which "true worshippers' shall worship God-the Father in spirit and in truth."

Isaiah 26:3 Thou will keep him in perfect peace, whose mind is stayed on thee: because he trusteth in thee.

Whenever our minds are stayed on the Lord Jesus, His peace will sustain and keep us in the right mood. It should be the desire of every believer to want to live in the very presence of God. He cares for His children. This is why we must make an effort to daily live in an attitude of Praise and Worship. God created us to walk and live in perfect harmony with Him.

CHAPTER 4

The Word Of God Speaks-Aug.17, 1985

I believe that fellowship, Communion, prayer, personal devotion, corporate worship, and witnessing or testifying about the grace of God in our hearts will create and standard of righteousness. When this does occur in our lives individually, then we will all begin to attend our church services with a new zeal for the Lord. Church is place and time for the Christian Believer or follower of Jesus Christ to find solace on common ground.

Isaiah 53:1 Who hath believed our report? And to whom is the arm of the LORD revealed? 2 For he shall grow up before him as a tender plant, and as a root out of a dry ground: he hath no form nor comeliness; and when we shall see him, there is no beauty that we should desire him.

3 He is despised and rejected of men; a man of sorrows, and acquainted with grief: and we hid as it were our faces from him; he was despised, and we esteemed him not.4 Surely he hath borne our griefs, and carried our sorrows: yet we did esteem him stricken, smitten of God, and afflicted. 5 But he was wounded for our transgressions, he was bruised for our iniquities: the chastisement of our peace was upon him; and with his stripes we are healed. I was meditating in Isaiah 53 approximately 12:40PM. The Word of the Lord was ministering to my spirit, soul, and mind: "Lord I want to identify with your death, burial, and resurrection.

Let me walk exactly where you walked and help me to respond with a Christ-Like attitude. Jesus, thank you for the price you paid on the cross. You had to endure cruel sufferings and you also accepted the penalty for my sin, which was death! Lord, you did all of this out of a genuine love for me. I love you Jesus.

2 Chronicles 35: 1 Moreover Josiah kept a passover unto the LORD in Jerusalem: and they killed the passover on the fourteenth day of the first month.2 And he set the priests in their charges, and encouraged them to the service of the house of the LORD, 3 And said unto the Levites that taught all Israel, which were

holy unto the LORD, Put the holy ark in the house which Solomon the son of David king of Israel did build; it shall not be a burden upon your shoulders: serve now the LORD your God, and his people Israel.

As I read these verses the Lord was speaking to my heart concerning His Church. "…Serve now the Lord your God, and His people Israel." Through Jesus Christ, all believers have become the true Israel of God. We are the spiritual seed of Abraham.

2 Chronicles 35:4 And prepare yourselves by the houses of your fathers, after your courses, according to the writing of David king of Israel, and according to the writing of Solomon his son. 5 And stand in the holy place according to the divisions of the families of the fathers of your brethren the people, and after the division of the families of the Levites.

6 So kill the passover, and sanctify yourselves, and prepare your brethren that they may do according to the word of the LORD by the hand of Moses.

This was the beginning of what I believe to be the preparation to attend International Bible College in San Antonio, Texas. God was conditioning my heart to become a vessel of honor in which He could use to minister the word of reconciliation. The will of God will be fulfilled in the earth. God is once again anointing His servants to declare His promises and empowering them to manifest His power in the land of the living. Expect great things such as: miracles, salvations, and blessings to be reported in the entire earth.

Philippians 3:3 New American Standard: for we are the [true] circumcision, who worship in the Spirit of God and glory in Christ Jesus and put no confidence in the flesh.

At the end of time there will be one nation of people from every tribe and race. They will be called the people of God, and will forever reign with Him. It's only through Jesus Christ that these citizens of heaven can have eternal access. No one will be able to boast about his or her own holiness or righteousness.

The redeemed of the Lord will dwell there. The blood of the Lamb has redeemed all the people back to fellowship with God. They have believed in the name of the beloved Son of God. I will be eternally grateful to be numbered with this holy race. May the blood of Jesus Christ forever cover me and wash away my sins.

I thank God that the finish work of grace at Calvary shows that God Almighty proved his love to us by sending His only beloved Son, Jesus. God did not send His Son to condemn us, but to show us the way back to the Father. He came to forgive us in such a way that we would desire "not to sin." The Lord sees the consequences that you will suffer by falling into sin. He gives us the grace to walk in perfect obedience to Him. The Holy Spirit will lead and guide us into all truth as we depend on God's Word.

CHAPTER 5

The Spiritual Battle

The Word of God Defends-Aug.18, 1985

There will never be a situation in our lives, when we fully trust the Lord, that He will allow us to be put to shame or confounded. Below is a sample of how the Word of God was speaking to my heart, mind, and spirit as I was consciously starting to say yes to the perfect will of God:

God will not allow the foot of the righteous to be moved. No weapon formed against us shall prosper. For greater is he that is in us, than he that is in the World. What shall we say to these things? If God is for us, who can be against us. [Psalm 121:2-3]Jn.4: 4,Isa.54: 17,Romans 8:31]

Therefore the child of God should always have an assurance in his heart that says, "God is with me. He has not abandoned me, or left me alone by myself." God is with us wherever we may go.

His name is Jehova-Shamah, which means the Lord is there. ref.Ezekiel 48:35 Also, there will never be a spiritual storm in our lives that Jesus cannot speak sweet peace and cause a gentle calmness that brings rest to the very soul and spirit of man. The peace of God can never be understood by the natural mind. But it keeps our hearts and minds on Christ.

2 Corinthians 10:3,4

"For the weapons of our warfare are not carnal but mighty in God for pulling down strongholds, casting down arguments and every high thing that exalts itself against the knowledge of God, bringing every thought into captivity to the obedience of Christ".

Never attempt to use the weapons of the flesh to defeat the Enemy. Simply recognize that you have power (dynamite-dunamis) and authority dwelling inside of you. God has always destined us to win whenever we depend on His awesome power enabling us to conquer every foe.

I have quoted these scriptures to combat the works of the Enemy. On August 18, 1985 I had an opportunity to compromise for a little while using the weapons of the flesh. I immediately recognized that this was wrong and asked Jesus to forgive me and help me to walk according to the spirit.

Acts 10:38 Anointed Jesus of Nazareth with the Holy Ghost and with power: who went about doing good, and healing all that were oppressed of the devil; for God was with him. Acts 1:5 For John truly baptized with water; but ye shall be baptized with the Holy Ghost not many days hence.

Isaiah 44:3-4For I will pour water upon him that is thirsty, and floods upon the dry ground: I will pour my spirit upon thy seed, and my blessing upon thine offspring:

Acts 2:4 And they were all filled with the Holy Ghost, and began to speak with other tongues, as the Spirit gave them utterance.

Acts 1:8 But ye shall receive power, after that the Holy Ghost is come upon you: and ye shall be witnesses unto me both in Jerusalem, and in all Judea, and in Samaria, and unto the uttermost part of the earth.

Acts 2:38Then Peter said unto them, Repent, and be baptized every one of you in the name of Jesus Christ for the remission of sins, and ye shall receive the gift of the Holy Ghost.

Acts 2:39 For the promise is unto you, and to your children, and to all that are afar off, even as many as the LORD our God shall call. Acts 4:31 And when they had prayed, the place was shaken where they were assembled together; and they were all filled with the Holy Ghost, and they spoke the word of God with boldness. Acts 6:3 Wherefore, brethren, look ye out among you seven men of honest report, full of the Holy Ghost and wisdom, whom we may appoint over this business. Acts 9:17 And Ananias went his way, and entered into the house; and putting his hands on him said, Brother Saul, the Lord, even Jesus, that appeared unto thee in the way as thou camest, hath sent me, that thou mightest receive thy sight, and be filled with the Holy Ghost.

The only way that every believer will be able to tear the work of Satan and build the Kingdom of God is through the empowering of the Holy Spirit. Ask God to fill you with His Holy Spirit from the innermost part of you. May you be filled with the Spirit of God.

If you have been easily getting angry and 'letting the Sun go down on your wrath' then you are living in the sin of condemnation. Condemnation comes directly from Satan himself. The enemy knows if he can keep you in a stubborn mood or attitude that you and I will never be able to hear what the Spirit is saying inside of you. God's Spirit ministers to our spirit. But we need to be still enough to hear that gentle voice of God.

Stop trying to defend yourself and begin to stand on the Word of God. God's Word is a double-edged sword that disciplines you and it also has the capability to drive back the powers of evil. After the Word of God chastises or corrects you, it leads you into an attitude of gratitude as you yield to the Lord. Remember, God is not angry or wanting to reject you. I can hear the voice of Jesus speaking to my heart: "My child, I love you and desire to have sweet communion with you. Allow my love to establish you with thoughts of unexplainable peace."

How can you fail when God is on you side? The Lord delivers us from every attack and temptation from our adversary, the devil. God's chosen servants are being released to do the will of God and fulfill the purposes of God in the Earth. The Lord is not allowing His children to go through trials without His divine protection.

In fact, the enemy cannot even touch us without full permission from our heavenly father. The devil must be exposed for telling lies to God's people. The Lord does have a purpose in allowing Satan to attack the believer. Even the devil had to receive permission to touch Job and his family. So begin to see what God is doing in your life and where He is leading you. I believe that the trial that we are facing or may face in the future are not even able to compared to the great blessings that God has prepared for the one who overcomes. There is a blessed reward awaiting the faithful child of God. Right before the answer or the victory comes Satan will revert to his old tricks and tell you that God has forgotten you, and that you're fighting this battle all by yourself! But lift up your voice and scream out-SATAN YOU ARE A LIAR!!! All who strive to live a holy life can expect that persecution will come. But God will defend you.

Romans 8:31 What shall we then say to these things? If God be for us, who can be against us? 32 He that spared not his own Son, but delivered him up for us all, how shall he not with him also freely give us all things? 33 Who shall lay any thing to the charge of God's elect? It is God that justifieth. 34 Who is he that condemneth? It is Christ that died, yea rather, that is risen again, who is even at the right hand of God, who also maketh intercession for us. 35 Who shall separate us from the love of Christ? Shall tribulation, or distress, or persecution, or famine, or nakedness, or peril, or sword? 36 As it is written, for thy sake we are killed all the day long; we are accounted as sheep for the slaughter. 37 Nay, in all these things we are more than conquerors through him that loved us.

38 For I am persuaded, that neither death, nor life, nor angels, nor principalities, nor powers, nor things present, nor things to come, 39 Nor height, nor depth, nor any other creature, shall be able to separate us from the love of God, which is in Christ Jesus our Lord.

CHAPTER 6

God's Provision-A Heart Of Gratitude

One thing that I am beginning to notice in my family is a spirit of giving. Almost every time that I would approach my sisters for anything, they gave me whatever they had. I viewed this as a sign that God was working in their hearts and minds. During this particular time period, I received a special gift from the Christian T.V. show called, *Praise The Lord,* which provoked me, to give immediately to help support the work of God.

I believe that every minister that may be having financial or spiritual problems in their ministry should start giving and this will automatically cause the blessings of the Lord to be released in a super-natural manner.

Luke 6:38 Give, and it shall be given unto you; good measure, pressed down, and shaken together, and running over, shall men give into your bosom. For with the same measure that ye mete withal it shall be measured to you again.

Prove God whenever you are struggling and minister to someone who is facing the same problem and you both will be delivered in due season. Trust in God and continue to good, and you will inherit the blessings of the Lord. Plant a good seed and expect to receive a harvest. I guarantee you on the authority and promises in the Word of God that you will receive more than enough! God is faithful to fulfill His promises when we come to him in faith believing that He is able to do what he has promised.

Always keep a song in your heart and let it be a song of praise unto the Lord. The Lord takes delight in seeing His children free in the spirit. Continue to rejoice and sing about the goodness of God. Jesus is so patient with us we are getting closer to seeing him face to face. The goodness of the Lord will lead us to repent and return to God. This is so important to remember that we are not saved by the good works we have done, but by the infinite mercy of a loving God who takes pleasure in blessing His children. We have been washed clean by the precious blood of the Lamb. Just thinking about this truth gives us a reason to thank the Lord with a heart of gratitude.

Never allow the joy of the Lord to be taken away from you. God's joy strengthens your heart and causes your faith to grow. If your faith is growing then God is definitely pleased with you. When you know that Jesus loves you and that He is pleased with you, then you automatically feel comfortable about worshipping the Lord with songs of joy!

Let the redeemed of the Lord begin to declare the greatness of our God. May the saints of the Most High God rejoice and lift up the name of the Lord and He in return will lift you up. "Oh Lord, there is no one as great as you. I praise you for the sacrifice you freely gave at the cross. Thank you for my salvation and purpose in this Earth. Lord, use me to be a blessing to your people by encouraging them in word, and in song. Restore the sheep of your pasture. Let the sound of rejoicing be heard in their midst.

One of the hardest lessons to learn is God's timing. For when you know in your heart that "everything will be fine" because you have learned the secret of giving all of your concerns to the Lord, God will in return give you the victory and assurance that He is in full control of your life. His burden is always lighter than ours. The fruit of patience will manifest itself and you will start to grow spiritually. The writer (Solomon) of the Book of Ecclesiastes says, "God makes everything beautiful, in His time." So it really doesn't matter how long the process may be. Whenever the time is right from God's perspective, all that you have been praying for, will all of a sudden be in reality. You will be able to see and touch it.

Ecclesiastes 3:11 He hath made every thing beautiful in his time: also he hath set the world in their heart, so that no man can find out the work that God maketh from the beginning to the end.

Even before you start to pray, your answer is on the way. God knows exactly what you and I need before we ask Him. So stop complaining or doubting His Word. At this very moment, begin to praise and thank the Lord. For He alone is worthy to receive the glory, honor, and power.

God loves you. Declare to yourself on a regular basis, "God love me and I appreciate the free gift of salvation." He sent His gift from heaven above. God allowed Jesus, His Son, to be *sown* in the Earth as he hung upon the cross. God sowed Jesus on Calvary and we are the offspring or the end result. We are the very harvest in which Jesus was referring to in the Holy Scriptures.

John 4: 35-38

35 Do you not say, 'Four months more and then the harvest'? I tell you, open your eyes and look at the fields! They are ripe for harvest. 36 Even now the reaper draws his wages; even now he harvests the crop for eternal life, so that the sower

and the reaper may be glad together. 37 Thus the saying 'One sows and another reaps' is true. 38 I sent you to reap what you have not worked for. Others have done the hard work, and you have reaped the benefits of their labor."

God in His mercy provided a sacrifice that was designed to bring you out of your sin and bondage. Even when you did not have the strength to come to Him, because of the load of sin...he came to give you a new life through the power of His resurrection. The same Spirit, anointing, and power that raised Jesus from the grave is available to you today. While the World was in sin and transgression, God cared enough to send His Son to die and conquer sin, death, Hell, and the grave. If this act of mercy doesn't reveal or display the splendor of God's love, then we are hopelessly lost.

CHAPTER 7

God's Spirit Speaks Directly

Let me share with you a word the Lord gave me on August 21, 1985 at 1:00AM. The Lord says that great and mighty things are in store for those that wait for Him. For the Lord is doing a great work, a quick work that is very new to the expectancy of His creation.

Corinthians 2:9 says, But as it is written, Eye hath not seen, nor ear heard, neither have entered into the heart of man, the things which God hath prepared for them that love him.

Isaiah 42:5-10 says, 5 Thus saith God the LORD, he that created the heavens, and stretched them out; he that spread forth the earth, and that which cometh out of it; he that giveth breath unto the people upon it, and spirit to them that walk therein: 6 I the LORD have called thee in righteousness, and will hold thine hand, and will keep thee, and give thee for a covenant of the people, for a light of the Gentiles; 7 To open the blind eyes, to bring out the prisoners from the prison, and them that sit in darkness out of the prison house.

8 I am the LORD: that is my name: and my glory will I not give to another, neither my praise to graven images. 9 Behold, the former things are come to pass, and new things do I declare: before they spring forth I tell you of them. 10 Sing unto the LORD a new song, and his praise from the end of the earth, ye that go down to the sea, and all that is therein; the isles, and the inhabitants thereof.

So we find that the Prophet Isaiah caught a vision of what God is about to do in these last days. God will manifest His power in such a way that there will be no excuse for the unbeliever. Jeremiah was receiving revelation from the Lord and declared what I believe to be a 'rhemah word' from the Lord: Jeremiah 33: 3 Call unto me, and I will answer thee, and show thee great and mighty things, which thou knowest not.

August 21, 1985

We are about to experience a mighty move of the Spirit of God. This movement will cause the Church of the Lord Jesus Christ to "be the Church." More than ever before God is bringing the Church back to a life of being sensitive to the moving of the Spirit. In order to be used by the Holy Spirit, you must open your heart to him and allow the Spirit to 'have his way.' Whenever the Spirit of God is in control of your life, you can expect him to wake you up early in the morning to intercede. I believe that many prayer warriors can identify with what I am referring to. Sometimes a strange feeling may come over you causing you to want to cry for no apparent reason.

This is the groaning of the Spirit mentioned in the book of Romans, Chapter 8: Likewise the Spirit also helpeth our infirmities: for we know not what we should pray for as we ought: but the Spirit itself maketh intercession for us with groanings which cannot be uttered. In the same way the Spirit also helps our weakness; for we do not know how to pray as we should, but the Spirit Himself intercedes for us with groanings too deep for words (NASB @1995).

Whenever the Spirit of God begins to intercede through you, yield to him. God is trying to use you to pray for something in the present, past, or future. We don't have the human capacity to know all the facts or details. But what we do know is that a Spiritual Alarm is sounding off inside of us. Never ignore the tugging or pull of the Holy Spirit. Humbly say: "Lord whatever you are wanting to speak to me or trying to accomplish your will through me, I'm with you 100%. Lord if there is an individual in trouble and in need of prayer and counseling, I pray that you would minister to them now."

Here is a testimony revealing this Spiritual Truth: One day I was carrying a heavy burden for a very dear friend and I did not know why. But every time I would think about her, I would pray fervently in the Spirit believing God for victory in her life. Well, several days later we met at a Christian event. She said you are not going to believe what happened to me. I just got out of the hospital. I tried to end my life. As she was speaking the Holy Spirit immediately quickened me and said, "This is why I laid her on your heart and allowed you to carry a heavy burden, and she won the battle and God gave her the victory."

'Because I stepped out in faith to obey the dealings of the Holy Spirit, a child of God was saved and delivered. Ask God to help you to be more sensitive to the voice of the Holy Spirit. There is nothing that God cannot do through the Spirit, if we would just yield ourselves to Him.

2 Chronicles 7:14

If my people, which are called by my name, shall humble themselves, and pray, and seek my face, and turn from their wicked ways; then will I hear from heaven, and will forgive their sin, and will heal their land.

Prayer is a mighty force that many of us are not using effectively. You must have a God-given desire to pray and be ready to see the benefits that comes as a result. When your prayer life affects those who are your enemies, then your prayer is effective. God sent the prophet Isaiah to tell Hezekiah to "get your house in order" because you are going to die. But then Hezekiah began to pray and present his case before the Lord and God heard from the heavens and sent Isaiah back to tell Hezekiah that 15 years has been added to his life.

Isaiah 38: 1 In those days was Hezekiah sick unto death. And Isaiah the prophet the son of Amoz came unto him, and said unto him, Thus saith the LORD, Set thine house in order: for thou shalt die, and not live. 2 Then Hezekiah turned his face toward the wall, and prayed unto the LORD, 3 And said, Remember now, O LORD, I beseech thee, how I have walked before thee in truth and with a perfect heart, and have done that which is good in thy sight. And Hezekiah wept sore.

4 Then came the word of the LORD to Isaiah, saying, 5 Go, and say to Hezekiah, Thus saith the LORD, the God of David thy father, I have heard thy prayer, I have seen thy tears: behold, I will add unto thy days fifteen years.

And I will deliver thee and this city out of the hand of the king of Assyria: and I will defend this city. 7 And this shall be a sign unto thee from the LORD, that the LORD will do this thing that he hath spoken; 8 Behold, I will bring again the shadow of the degrees, which is gone down in the sun dial of Ahaz, ten degrees backward. So the sun returned ten degrees, by which degrees it was gone down. 9 The writing of Hezekiah king of Judah, when he had been sick, and was recovered of his sickness: 10 I said in the cutting off of my days, I shall go to the gates of the grave: I am deprived of the residue of my years. 11 I said, I shall not see the LORD, even the LORD, in the land of the living: I shall behold man no more with the inhabitants of the world. 12 Mine age is departed, and is removed from me as a shepherd's tent. I have cut off like a weaver my life: he will cut me off with pining sickness: from day even to night wilt thou make an end of me.   13 I reckoned till morning, that, as a lion, so will he break all my bones: from day even to night wilt thou make an end of me. 14 Like a crane or a swallow, so did I chatter: I did mourn as a dove: mine eyes fail with looking upward: O LORD, I am oppressed; undertake for me. 15 What shall I say? He hath both spoken unto me, and himself hath done it: I shall go softly all my years in the bitterness of my soul.

16 O LORD, by these things men live, and in all these things is the life of my spirit: so wilt thou recover me, and make me to live. 17 Behold, for peace I had great bitterness: but thou hast in love to my soul delivered it from the pit of corruption: for thou hast cast all my sins behind thy back. 18 For the grave cannot praise thee, death cannot celebrate thee: they that go down into the pit cannot hope for thy truth. 19 The living, the living, he shall praise thee, as I do this day: the father to the children shall make known thy truth. 20 The LORD was ready to save me: therefore we will sing my songs to the stringed instruments all the days of our life in the house of the LORD. 21 For Isaiah had said, let them take a lump of figs, and lay it for a plaster upon the boil, and he shall recover. 22Hezekiah also had said, what is the sign that I shall go up to the house of the LORD?

Jesus emphatically states that his sheep can hear his voice. Therefore, it should never be such a mystery whenever a born-again believer declares that: "God is speaking to me" or that "the Holy Spirit has spoken to my heart." The bible emphatically states in John 10: 1-4 "Verily, verily, I say unto you, He that entereth not by the door into the sheepfold, but climbeth up some other way, the same is a thief and a robber. 2 But he that entereth in by the door is the shepherd of the sheep. 3 To him the porter openeth; and the sheep hear his voice: and he calleth his own sheep by name, and leadeth them out. 4 And when he putteth forth his own sheep, he goeth before them, and the sheep follow him: for they know his voice.

CHAPTER 8

Prayer Is The Key

We must become bold in our prayers and declare that we are going to remain steadfast in faith believing until the answer comes. I choose to seek the Lord and hold on until He blesses me. Do not worry about what people say. Refuse to give up until you see complete victory. Fight the good fight of faith. The people that hurt you the most are the ones that you love. Remember that God will begin to answer our prayers when we pray for those who persecute us. Jesus prayed that the will of God be done. He could have called legion of angels to destroy all his enemies. Yet He prayed Father forgive them, for they know not what they do or have done. Pray for your enemies according to the scriptures that God will bless them.

The greatest power that the World knows is at your fingertips by praying Prayer is a force that cannot me be stopped. Heaven cannot turn a deaf ear when you begin to pray. Whenever Moses sought the face of God, the Lord appeared unto him. God could not ignore Moses' prayer.

He interceded for the children of Israel and also, for Miriam and Aaron when God was angry at the rebellion of His people. If Moses would not have stood in the gap before the Lord on behalf of the children of Israel and also for Aaron and Miriam, God probably would have destroyed them all and chose another group of people to enter into a covenant with Him. This shows us the power of prayer in our lives.

Prayer can change the heart and mind of God. You need to PUSH, pray until something happens. If you would learn to pray through, there is nothing that God can't change or alter. You will come out of the problem victorious and the people around you will know that the Lord God in your life is great! Now is the time to become valiant and not to give up.

Matthew 11: Verily I say unto you, Among them that are born of women there hath not risen a greater than John the Baptist: notwithstanding he that is least in the kingdom of heaven is greater than he.

The devil thinks that he's going to intimidate the Church! It is time for us to let the devil know that, "I am not afraid." The disciples knew why Jesus could do great and mighty things, because of Jesus' prayer life. You will not see the results that you asking from God until you pray in faith believing God to do what he has promised.

Isaiah 49:8 Thus saith the LORD, In an acceptable time have I heard thee, and in a day of salvation have I helped thee: and I will preserve thee, and give thee for a covenant of the people, to establish the earth, to cause to inherit the desolate heritages; 9 That thou mayest say to the prisoners, Go forth; to them that [are] in darkness, Shew yourselves. They shall feed in the ways, and their pastures [shall be] in all high places. 10 They shall not hunger nor thirst; neither shall the heat nor sun smite them: for he that hath mercy on them shall lead them, even by the springs of water shall he guide them. 11 And I will make all my mountains a way, and my highways shall be exalted.

"God is saying to me through these verses: I will make all my mountains … I put them there. They are my mountains and I willed it around for your victory! That which is in front of you sometimes seems impossible. But the Lord is saying to me: don't worry, because I will make a highway for you to be able to go through those mountains.

Jeremiah 33:3-14 shall be fulfilled very shortly. The Lord is getting ready to restore all things that were stolen away from His people. There shall be more healings greater than the ones that have been recorded. This is beginning to take place even now. The youth shall carry the torch of the gospel of Jesus Christ, being empowered, filled, controlled, and led by the Spirit of the Lord. For God's Spirit shall be poured out in these Last Days and those who are expecting great things shall experience it."

Isaiah 49:16 Behold, I have graven thee upon the palms of [my] hands; thy walls [are] continually before me. The Lord is reminding me that I am in the palm of His hands. He is telling me that He loves me and did not forget me. Those scars in the hands of Jesus can never be removed. Whenever Jesus looks at His hands, he sees me there.

Isaiah 53:3-5 He is despised and rejected of men; a man of sorrows, and acquainted with grief: and we hid as it were [our] faces from him; he was despised, and we esteemed him not. 4 Surely he hath borne our grief, and carried our sorrows: yet we did esteem him stricken, smitten of God, and afflicted. 5 But he [was] wounded for our transgressions, [he was] bruised for our iniquities: the chastisement of our peace [was] upon him; and with his stripes we are healed.

John1: 11-13 He came unto his own, and his own received him not. 12 But as many as received him, to them gave he power to become the sons of God, [even] to them that believe on his name: 13 Which were born, not of blood, nor of the will of the flesh, nor of the will of man, but of God.

I can sort of relate to Jesus how He left the portals of glory and entered into this World to bring a message of hope to His people. But they refused to listen and hardened their hearts. They literally rejected the message of God. Their attitude reflected these words: "We don't need a Savior. We do not want a message of love. But we want a message of dictatorship. If you are the really Son of God, why did this or that happen to me or to someone close to me? We want to lead our own lives. Go tell it to somebody that really needs to hear it."

Acts 16: 25-31

25And at midnight Paul and Silas prayed, and sang praises unto God: and the prisoners heard them. 26And suddenly there was a great earthquake, so that the foundations of the prison were shaken: and immediately all the doors were opened, and every one's bands were loosed.

27And the keeper of the prison awaking out of his sleep, and seeing the prison doors open, he drew out his sword, and would have killed himself, supposing that the prisoners had been fled. 28But Paul cried with a loud voice, saying, Do thyself no harm: for we are all here. 29Then he called for a light, and sprang in, and came trembling, and fell down before Paul and Silas, 30And brought them out, and said, Sirs, what must I do to be saved? 31And they said, Believe on the Lord Jesus Christ, and thou shalt be saved, and thy house.

Paul and Silas began to pray to the Lord and sang praises in spirit and in truth. The bible declares that the other prisoners heard them. After they approached the throne room of heaven and had a tremendous encounter with God, the prisoners, also received the victory that they received from the Lord. All of their chains and bonds were loosed and they were set free. If Paul and Silas had chosen to complain about being put into stocks and bonds, they would have never been able to pray effectively. The bible states that God inhabits the praises of His people. They certainly had to have insight into this key to victory. Prayer and praise must be coupled together in order for a mighty revival to touch the Earth.

Our prayers will work in the prisons, hospitals, schools, colleges, and any other place that is available to receive a miracle from God. God is dealing with

His creation to come back to total dependency on the Creator. There is a time coming to the World you are living in today, in which the rulers of the land will have to come to the Church (the born-again, Spirit filled. Spirit led servants of God) for all answers of life's problems. God will use His people to pull down the strongholds through intercessory prayer in the Spirit. There are certain situations that will require more anointing and power in order to produce spiritual results. God commands us to continue praying and not to be discouraged if the answer does not come quickly. Prayer will change us and then affect the circumstances around us.

CHAPTER 9

The Boldness Of The Spirit-September 1985

We have boldness through the power of the Holy Spirit. The Word of God should never be spoken without the unction of the Spirit of God. The gospel of Jesus Christ has the power to set the captives free. It really doesn't matter what the stronghold may be called: Drug Addiction, Lust, Pornography, Anger, Fear, Personality Disorders, Cancer, All Sicknesses, or Personal Financial Problems, because I know that one touch from the presence of God will eradicate all of these problems and more.

There are billions of lives that have been transformed as a result of hearing the gospel declared and accepting Jesus Christ as personal Lord and Savior. This is actually an endorsement that salvation comes from God and is experienced anywhere on the Earth. The last words of Jesus to His disciples was a commandment to Go into all the World and take this message of love to everyone who is lost in sin.

Matthew 28:19-20

19 Go ye therefore, and teach all nations, baptizing them in the name of the Father, and of the Son, and of the Holy Ghost: 20 Teaching them to observe all things whatsoever I have commanded you: and, lo, I am with you always, even unto the end of the world. Amen.

Romans 1:16 For I am not ashamed of the gospel of Christ: for it is the power of God unto salvation to every one that believeth; to the Jew first, and also to the Greek. 17 For therein is the righteousness of God revealed from faith to faith: as it is written, the just shall live by faith.

I believe a holy boldness is about to be manifested in thousands of God's people. We, the Church are tired of being pushed around by the devil. Jesus gave us all power and authority over the Enemy. The Church has been empowered with a God-given ability to fight back using the power of God, which is the anointing of the Holy Spirit.

Jeremiah 31:11 For the LORD hath redeemed Jacob, and ransomed him from the hand of him that was stronger than he. God is our side and we therefore have an assurance that we will not be defeated. The battle does not belong to us; the battle belongs to the Lord.

At one time the devil had a lot of power, but when Jesus died and was buried, He arose three days later with all power in His hands.

Luke 10:19

19 Behold, I give unto you power to tread on serpents and scorpions, and over all the power of the enemy: and nothing shall by any means hurt you.

This scripture has divine insight for the power in which the Lord delegated to His Church, the body of Christ. This power is to be used for combat against the forces of the evil one: the devil. God never intended for a believer to go around boasting about how spiritual they are.

The Bible teaches that I am what I am, but by the grace of God and not by my own efforts. The boldness that I am referring to is the confidence that God placed in the heart of every child of God upon receiving Jesus Christ. It is so easy to believe the Word of God and trust in all of the promises, when you know that your very name is written in the Lamb's book of life.

Jeremiah 31:

12 Therefore they shall come and sing in the height of Zion, and shall flow together to the goodness of the LORD, for wheat, and for wine, and for oil, and for the young of the flock and of the herd: and their soul shall be as a watered garden; and they shall not sorrow any more at all.

How can we worry when we know that Jesus is interceding (praying) for us at this very moment! Jesus made a declaration that His church will be built and that the powers of the enemy would not be able to stop it. So the Church belongs to the Lord. He is the boss, the one that calls all of the shots. He gives the orders and direction to the Body of Christ.

The Church is being guilt upon a rock: that rock is a revelation and understanding of who Jesus really is. He is the Christ, the Son of the Living God, The Great I AM, Almighty and Powerful God! Remember it was the desire of Jesus Christ to make him known to the people of His day. Instead, he gave the job to his followers: those disciples who tarried in the Upper Room until they were filled with Divine power from on high.

Matthew 28: 18And Jesus came and spake unto them, saying, all power is given unto me in heaven and in earth. 19Go ye therefore, and teach all nations, baptizing them in the name of the Father, and of the Son, and of the Holy Ghost:

20Teaching them to observe all things whatsoever I have commanded you: and, lo, I am with you always, even unto the end of the world. Amen. The Church is being conformed into the very image of Jesus Christ. Jesus said that we shall do greater works than what he had already accomplished in the Earth. He was going back to the Father and would send the Holy Spirit to equip and motivate us to share the love of God with those who feel unloved and feel like no one cares. But we who have experienced God's forgiving power knows that Jesus truly satisfies the longing soul with inner peace and blessed assurance. Jesus Christ is the answer.

CHAPTER 10

Prophecies From New Orleans

These are the days that the prophets of the Old Testament have longed to look into or be apart of. Let me share with you exactly what I received from the scriptures to be a Word from the Lord. I lived in New Orleans, Louisiana most of my life as a child from May 11, 1965 (birth date) until January 6, 1986 (entry date for International Bible College). This is my foundational scripture that the Lord led me to in 1984 while living in New Orleans, Louisiana: Luke 22:31And the Lord said, Simon, Simon, behold, Satan hath desired to have you, that he may sift you as wheat: 32But I have prayed for thee, that thy faith fail not: and when thou art converted, strengthen thy brethren. I am determine more than ever before to fulfill my purpose in the Earth. Here are prophecies from New Orleans to the World. We are living in perilous times and glorious days.

On September 11, 1985 The Lord released this word: Go forward and posses the land… For the spirit of God will say go forward and possess the land. I have called you to finish the work of the Lord. Yes, I will be with you always as I am with you even now. Fear no longer, for I am walking across with you. Go over to the other side. The blessings of the Lord are waiting for you. Step out. Yes I say unto you to step out with the presence of the Lord.

October 1985-The Lord released this word to me as I was praying about which Bible College to attend: My son, I am reminding you of my Word to your heart. Let not my truth forsake you. Hold on to my word. It will keep you from falling or from ever becoming discouraged. Be thou strong in the Lord and allow my love to grip your heart. My son, I desire have fellowship with you. So come aside for a while and spend time in my presence. The more you stay in my presence, the more you will know that you are my son and that I am with you whenever you have a problem.

Many of your Christian brothers and sisters are discouraged. Go out and
"Strengthen thy brethren" as I have shown you in time past. Be that example that
I called you to be. But remember, you must spend time worshipping and praising
me, says the Spirit of God.

A Personal Prophetic Prayer To God-October 17, 1985

"Dear God, I pray in Jesus name that you will open up my vocal cords, so
that I can sing for you. Lord if you open my vocal cords and give me wisdom in
knowing how to use my voice, I will only use the songs that I sing to bring glory
to God in the highest. I will let the people to whom I am singing to, know that
your grace has kept me thus far and your mercy is allowing me to sing. I commit
my life to you, Lord. Jesus you are my everything, and thank you for hearing
my prayer. Use me to strengthen your people, and to feed your sheep and lambs.

They have been wounded in their spirit. Thank you for anointing me to sing
down the glory of God upon your children, who needs to be refreshed. I receive
this answer to prayer and I give my voice, my entire life to you Lord. Amen.
The Lord is letting me know that He is with me and His favor is upon my
life. It makes me feel so glad to know that my Heavenly Father is watching over
me. Lord you know if I am walking by faith or not. Help me to stand still and
see the salvation of the Lord. People, we must allow God to be God in our lives,
if we want to see the people around us getting saved. The sinners know if you
are genuine or if God is moving in your life. Praise God for his loving-kindness.
God cares about everything that affects us. We are His children, and God loves
you and me.
Thank you Lord for pouring your love upon us by your Spirit. Lord you truly
love people from all walks of life. Let the Earth declare His glory, for he is worthy
to be praised both now until Eternity. Jesus Christ is Lord of all. Bless His holy
name. Amen.
Prophecy From Isaiah 48: 6-13 (Rhemah Word)
6 Thou hast heard, see all this; and will not ye declare it? I have showed thee
new things from this time, even hidden things, and thou didst not know them.
7 They are created now, and not from the beginning; even before the day when
thou heardest them not; lest thou shouldest say, Behold, I knew them. 8 Yea, thou
heardest not; yea, thou knewest not; yea, from that time that thine ear was not
opened: for I knew that thou wouldest deal very treacherously, and was called a
transgressor from the womb. 9 For my name's sake will I defer mine anger, and
for my praise will I refrain for thee, that I cut thee not off.

10 Behold, I have refined thee, but not with silver; I have chosen thee in the furnace of affliction. 11 For mine own sake, even for mine own sake, will I do it: for how should my name be polluted? And I will not give my glory unto another. 12 Hearken unto me, O Jacob and Israel, my called; I am he; I am the first, I also am the last. 13Mine hand also hath laid the foundation of the earth, and my right hand hath spanned the heavens: when I call unto them, they stand up together.

The Spirit of God is speaking through the scriptures. We need to listen and obey the written word and the spoken Word of God. The Lord has chosen us to accomplish His purposes in the land.

Divine Revelation-September 26, 1985

More than ever before, God is unveiling His glory to the Church. It is the same glory that was seen upon Moses whenever he came out of the mount after talking with God. The same glory that filled Solomon's Temple is filling our spiritual temple. God sent the former rain on the Day of Pentecost in the Upper Room.

The word of God says that we are the temple of the Holy Spirit. The glory or anointing that rested upon our Lord when He was transfigured before Peter, James, and John has been given to the true body of the Lord Jesus Christ. We will know that we know that Jesus is God. He is the answer to all of man's problems. The Holy Spirit is waiting to talk to you and me about Jesus and the Father. Yield to him right now. God desires to know you. He wants you to know him. Whenever you receive this revelation in the knowledge of Him, you will never be the same. You have found your destiny.

Isaiah 65:16-20 (Rhemah Word)

16That he who blesseth himself in the earth shall bless himself in the God of truth; and he that sweareth in the earth shall swear by the God of truth; because the former troubles are forgotten, and because they are hid from mine eyes. **17** For, behold, I create new heavens and a new earth: and the former shall not be remembered, nor come into mind. **18** But be ye glad and rejoice for ever in that which I create: for, behold, I create Jerusalem a rejoicing, and her people a joy. **19** And I will rejoice in Jerusalem, and joy in my people: and the voice of weeping shall be no more heard in her, nor the voice of crying.

Isaiah 66:10 Rejoice ye with Jerusalem, and be glad with her, all ye that love her: rejoice for joy with her, all ye that mourn for her: 12 For thus saith the LORD, Behold, I will extend peace to her like a river, and the glory of the Gentiles like a flowing stream: then shall ye suck, ye shall be borne upon her sides, and be dandled upon her knees.

Jeremiah 29: 11-14 (Rhemah Word)

11 For I know the plans that I have for you,' declares the LORD, 'plans for welfare and not for calamity to give you a future and a hope. 12 Then you will call upon Me and come and pray to Me, and I will listen to you. 13 You will seek Me and find Me when you search for Me with all your heart. 14 I will be found by you,' declares the LORD, 'and I will restore your fortunes and will gather you from all the nations and from all the places where I have driven you,' declares the LORD, 'and I will bring you back to the place from where I sent you into exile.'

Jeremiah 30

1The word that came to Jeremiah from the LORD, saying, 2Thus speaketh the LORD God of Israel, saying, Write thee all the words that I have spoken unto thee in a book. 3For, lo, the days come, saith the LORD, that I will bring again the captivity of my people Israel and Judah, saith the LORD: and I will cause them to return to the land that I gave to their fathers, and they shall possess it. 4And these are the words that the LORD spake concerning Israel and concerning Judah. 5For thus saith the LORD; We have heard a voice of trembling, of fear, and not of peace.

6Ask ye now, and see whether a man doth travail with child? wherefore do I see every man with his hands on his loins, as a woman in travail, and all faces are turned into paleness? 7Alas! for that day is great, so that none is like it: it is even the time of Jacob's trouble, but he shall be saved out of it. 8 For it shall come to pass in that day, saith the LORD of hosts, that I will break his yoke from off thy neck, and will burst thy bonds, and strangers shall no more serve themselves of him: 9But they shall serve the LORD their God, and David their king, whom I will raise up unto them. 10Therefore fear thou not, O my servant Jacob, saith the LORD; neither be dismayed, O Israel: for, lo, I will save thee from afar, and thy seed from the land of their captivity; and Jacob shall return, and shall be in rest, and be quiet, and none shall make him afraid. 11For I am with thee, saith the LORD, to save thee: though I make a full end of all nations whither I have scattered thee, yet I will not make a full end of thee: but I will correct thee in measure, and will not leave thee altogether unpunished.

12For thus saith the LORD, Thy bruise is incurable, and thy wound is grievous. 13There is none to plead thy cause, that thou mayest be bound up: thou hast no healing medicines. 14All thy lovers have forgotten thee; they seek thee not; for I have wounded thee with the wound of an enemy, with the chastisement of a cruel one, for the multitude of thine iniquity; because thy sins were increased.

15Why criest thou for thine affliction? thy sorrow is incurable for the multitude of thine iniquity: because thy sins were increased, I have done these things unto thee. 16Therefore all they that devour thee shall be devoured; and all thine adversaries, every one of them, shall go into captivity; and they that spoil thee shall be a spoil, and all that prey upon thee will I give for a prey. 17For I will restore health unto thee, and I will heal thee of thy wounds, saith the LORD; because they called thee an Outcast, saying, This is Zion, whom no man seeketh after. 18Thus saith the LORD; Behold, I will bring again the captivity of Jacob's tents, and have mercy on his dwellingplaces; and the city shall be builded upon her own heap, and the palace shall remain after the manner thereof. 19And out of them shall proceed thanksgiving and the voice of them that make merry: and I will multiply them, and they shall not be few; I will also glorify them, and they shall not be small. 20Their children also shall be as aforetime, and their congregation shall be established before me, and I will punish all that oppress them. 21And their nobles shall be of themselves, and their governor shall proceed from the midst of them; and I will cause him to draw near, and he shall approach unto me: for who is this that engaged his heart to approach unto me? saith the LORD.

22And ye shall be my people, and I will be your God. 23Behold, the whirlwind of the LORD goeth forth with fury, a continuing whirlwind: it shall fall with pain upon the head of the wicked. 24The fierce anger of the LORD shall not return, until he hath done it, and until he have performed the intents of his heart: in the latter days ye shall consider it.

Jeremiah 31 (Rhemah Word)

1At the same time, saith the LORD, will I be the God of all the families of Israel, and they shall be my people. 2Thus saith the LORD, The people which were left of the sword found grace in the wilderness; even Israel, when I went to cause him to rest.

3The LORD hath appeared of old unto me, saying, Yea, I have loved thee with an everlasting love: therefore with lovingkindness have I drawn thee. 4Again I will build thee, and thou shalt be built, O virgin of Israel: thou shalt again be adorned with thy tabrets, and shalt go forth in the dances of them that make merry. 5Thou shalt yet plant vines upon the mountains of Samaria: the planters shall plant, and shall eat them as common things. 6For there shall be a day, that the watchmen upon the mount Ephraim shall cry, Arise ye, and let us go up to Zion unto the LORD our God.

7For thus saith the LORD; Sing with gladness for Jacob, and shout among the chief of the nations: publish ye, praise ye, and say, O LORD, save thy people, the remnant of Israel. 8Behold, I will bring them from the north country, and gather them from the coasts of the earth, and with them the blind and the lame, the woman with child and her that travaileth with child together: a great company shall return thither. 9They shall come with weeping, and with supplications will I lead them: I will cause them to walk by the rivers of waters in a straight way, wherein they shall not stumble: for I am a father to Israel, and Ephraim is my firstborn. 10Hear the word of the LORD, O ye nations, and declare it in the isles afar off, and say, He that scattered Israel will gather him, and keep him, as a shepherd doth his flock. 11For the LORD hath redeemed Jacob, and ransomed him from the hand of him that was stronger than he. 12Therefore they shall come and sing in the height of Zion, and shall flow together to the goodness of the LORD, for wheat, and for wine, and for oil, and for the young of the flock and of the herd: and their soul shall be as a watered garden; and they shall not sorrow any more at all.

13Then shall the virgin rejoice in the dance, both young men and old together: for I will turn their mourning into joy, and will comfort them, and make them rejoice from their sorrow. 14And I will satiate the soul of the priests with fatness, and my people shall be satisfied with my goodness, saith the LORD. 15Thus saith the LORD; A voice was heard in Ramah, lamentation, and bitter weeping; Rahel weeping for her children refused to be comforted for her children, because they were not. 16Thus saith the LORD; Refrain thy voice from weeping, and thine eyes from tears: for thy work shall be rewarded, saith the LORD; and they shall come again from the land of the enemy. 17And there is hope in thine end, saith the LORD, that thy children shall come again to their own border.

18 I have surely heard Ephraim bemoaning himself thus; Thou hast chastised me, and I was chastised, as a bullock unaccustomed to the yoke: turn thou me, and I shall be turned; for thou art the LORD my God. 19 Surely after that I was turned, I repented; and after that I was instructed, I smote upon my thigh: I was ashamed, yea, even confounded, because I did bear the reproach of my youth.

20 Is Ephraim my dear son? is he a pleasant child? for since I spake against him, I do earnestly remember him still: therefore my bowels are troubled for him; I will surely have mercy upon him, saith the LORD. 21Set thee up waymarks, make thee high heaps: set thine heart toward the highway, even the way which thou wentest: turn again, O virgin of Israel, turn again to these thy cities. 22How long wilt thou go about, O thou backsliding daughter? for the LORD hath created a new thing in the earth, A woman shall compass a man.

23Thus saith the LORD of hosts, the God of Israel; As yet they shall use this speech in the land of Judah and in the cities thereof, when I shall bring again their captivity; The LORD bless thee, O habitation of justice, and mountain of holiness. 24And there shall dwell in Judah itself, and in all the cities thereof together, husbandmen, and they that go forth with flocks. 25For I have satiated the weary soul, and I have replenished every sorrowful soul. 26Upon this I awaked, and beheld; and my sleep was sweet unto me. 27Behold, the days come, saith the LORD, that I will sow the house of Israel and the house of Judah with the seed of man, and with the seed of beast.

28And it shall come to pass, that like as I have watched over them, to pluck up, and to break down, and to throw down, and to destroy, and to afflict; so will I watch over them, to build, and to plant, saith the LORD. 29In those days they shall say no more, The fathers have eaten a sour grape, and the children's teeth are set on edge. 30But every one shall die for his own iniquity: every man that eateth the sour grape, his teeth shall be set on edge. 31Behold, the days come, saith the LORD, that I will make a new covenant with the house of Israel, and with the house of Judah:

32 Not according to the covenant that I made with their fathers in the day that I took them by the hand to bring them out of the land of Egypt; which my covenant they brake, although I was an husband unto them, saith the LORD: 33But this shall be the covenant that I will make with the house of Israel; After those days, saith the LORD, I will put my law in their inward parts, and write it in their hearts; and will be their God, and they shall be my people.

34And they shall teach no more every man his neighbour, and every man his brother, saying, Know the LORD: for they shall all know me, from the least of them unto the reatest of them, saith the LORD: for I will forgive their iniquity, and I will remember their sin no more. 35Thus saith the LORD, which giveth the sun for a light by day, and the ordinances of the moon and of the stars for a light by night, which divideth the sea when the waves thereof roar; The LORD of hosts is his name: 36If those ordinances depart from before me, saith the LORD, then the seed of Israel also shall cease from being a nation before me for ever.

37Thus saith the LORD; If heaven above can be measured, and the foundations of the earth searched out beneath, I will also cast off all the seed of Israel for all that they have done, saith the LORD. 38Behold, the days come, saith the LORD, that the city shall be built to the LORD from the tower of Hananeel unto the gate of the corner. 39And the measuring line shall yet go forth over against it upon the hill Gareb, and shall compass about to Goath. 40And the whole valley of the dead bodies, and of the ashes, and all the fields unto the brook of Kidron, unto the corner of the horse gate toward the east, shall be holy unto the LORD; it shall not be plucked up, nor thrown down any more for ever.

Jeremiah 32:27Behold, I am the LORD, the God of all flesh: is there any thing too hard for me?

Jeremiah 33: 1 Moreover the word of the LORD came unto Jeremiah the second time, while he was yet shut up in the court of the prison, saying, 2Thus saith the LORD the maker thereof, the LORD that formed it, to establish it; the LORD is his name; 3Call unto me, and I will answer thee, and show thee great and mighty things, which thou knowest not. 4For thus saith the LORD, the God of Israel, concerning the houses of this city, and concerning the houses of the kings of Judah, which are thrown down by the mounts, and by the sword; 5They come to fight with the Chaldeans, but it is to fill them with the dead bodies of men, whom I have slain in mine anger and in my fury, and for all whose wickedness I have hid my face from this city. 6Behold, I will bring it health and cure, and I will cure them, and will reveal unto them the abundance of peace and truth.

7And I will cause the captivity of Judah and the captivity of Israel to return, and will build them, as at the first. 8And I will cleanse them from all their iniquity, whereby they have sinned against me; and I will pardon all their iniquities, whereby they have sinned, and whereby they have transgressed against me. 9And it shall be to me a name of joy, a praise and an honour before all the nations of the earth, which shall hear all the good that I do unto them: and they shall fear and tremble for all the goodness and for all the prosperity that I procure unto it. 10Thus saith the LORD; Again there shall be heard in this place, which ye say shall be desolate without man and without beast, even in the cities of Judah, and in the streets of Jerusalem, that are desolate, without man, and without inhabitant, and without beast, 11The voice of joy, and the voice of gladness, the voice of the bridegroom, and the voice of the bride, the voice of them that shall say, Praise the LORD of hosts: for the LORD is good; for his mercy endureth for ever: and of them that shall bring the sacrifice of praise into the house of the LORD. For I will cause to return the captivity of the land, as at the first, saith the LORD. 12Thus saith the LORD of hosts; Again in this place, which is desolate without man and without beast, and in all the cities thereof, shall be an habitation of shepherds causing their flocks to lie down. 13In the cities of the mountains, in the cities of the vale, and in the cities of the south, and in the land of Benjamin, and in the places about Jerusalem, and in the cities of Judah, shall the flocks pass again under the hands of him that telleth them, saith the LORD.

14Behold, the days come, saith the LORD, that I will perform that good thing which I have promised unto the house of Israel and to the house of Judah. 15In those days, and at that time, will I cause the Branch of righteousness to grow up unto David; and he shall execute judgment and righteousness in the land. 16In those days shall Judah be saved, and Jerusalem shall dwell safely: and this is the name wherewith she shall be called, The LORD our righteousness. 17For thus saith the LORD; David shall never want a man to sit upon the throne of the house of Israel;

18Neither shall the priests the Levites want a man before me to offer burnt offerings, and to kindle meat offerings, and to do sacrifice continually. 19And the word of the LORD came unto Jeremiah, saying, 20 Thus saith the LORD; If ye can break my covenant of the day, and my covenant of the night, and that there should not be day and night in their season; 21Then may also my covenant be broken with David my servant, that he should not have a son to reign upon his throne; and with the Levites the priests, my ministers.

22As the host of heaven cannot be numbered, neither the sand of the sea measured: so will I multiply the seed of David my servant, and the Levites that minister unto me.

The prevailing message that I received from the Lord that there was coming destruction, devastation, and glorious restoration in the last days. God is raising me up to bring a word of reconciliation to His people. Go out into the World and minister to God's people through preaching, prayer, and worship. As the years have passed, my understanding is much clearer to what my purpose and calling is all about in the kingdom of God. The enemy of our souls will do his best to use the ones that are the closes to us. He knows that if you and I can allow the cares of life get the best of us, or hinder us, that the purposes of God for us could be in jeopardy.

So right now you have to determine with all that is inside of you, that you will not bow down to the spirit of rejection. There is a price that you have to pay. Be willing to be hated or rejected by the World, by your friends and family members. Somehow, I am convinced that God has a greater calling, a greater blessing, and a greater anointing to be poured out upon the lives of the obedient children of God.

We have to make a choice as to who or what we are going to serve.

The World has many options for us to choose from. But God's way leads to life, and man's ways will lead to eternal damnation.

My utmost heartbeat is resounding: "I will serve the Lord with all of my heart, soul, mind, and strength." Souls are depending on your obedience to God. There are people who have never accepted Jesus Christ as their Savior and Lord. Your obedience will cause lost souls to be able to come into the Kingdom of God for the very first time. In addition, backsliders will return to God and walk in perfect harmony with the will of God. The book of Isaiah reveals the heart of God for His people. God demands and desires that we obey His command-ments in order to receive divine blessings that will affect us spirit-ually, physically, financially, emotionally, and materially. There is always a condition: Isaiah 1:19 If you will only obey me, you will have plenty to eat. 20 But if you turn away and refuse to listen, you will be devoured by the sword of your enemies. I, the LORD, have spoken!"(**New Living Translation)**